THE NATIONAL PARKS ART BOOK

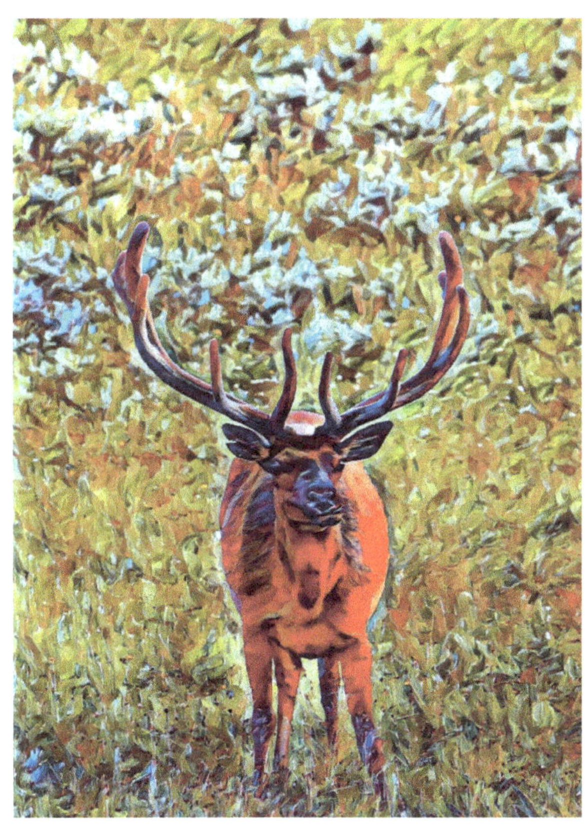

By Livingcolors Publishing

A FREE GIFT FOR YOU!

Download Art Images for Free!

For those that love nature

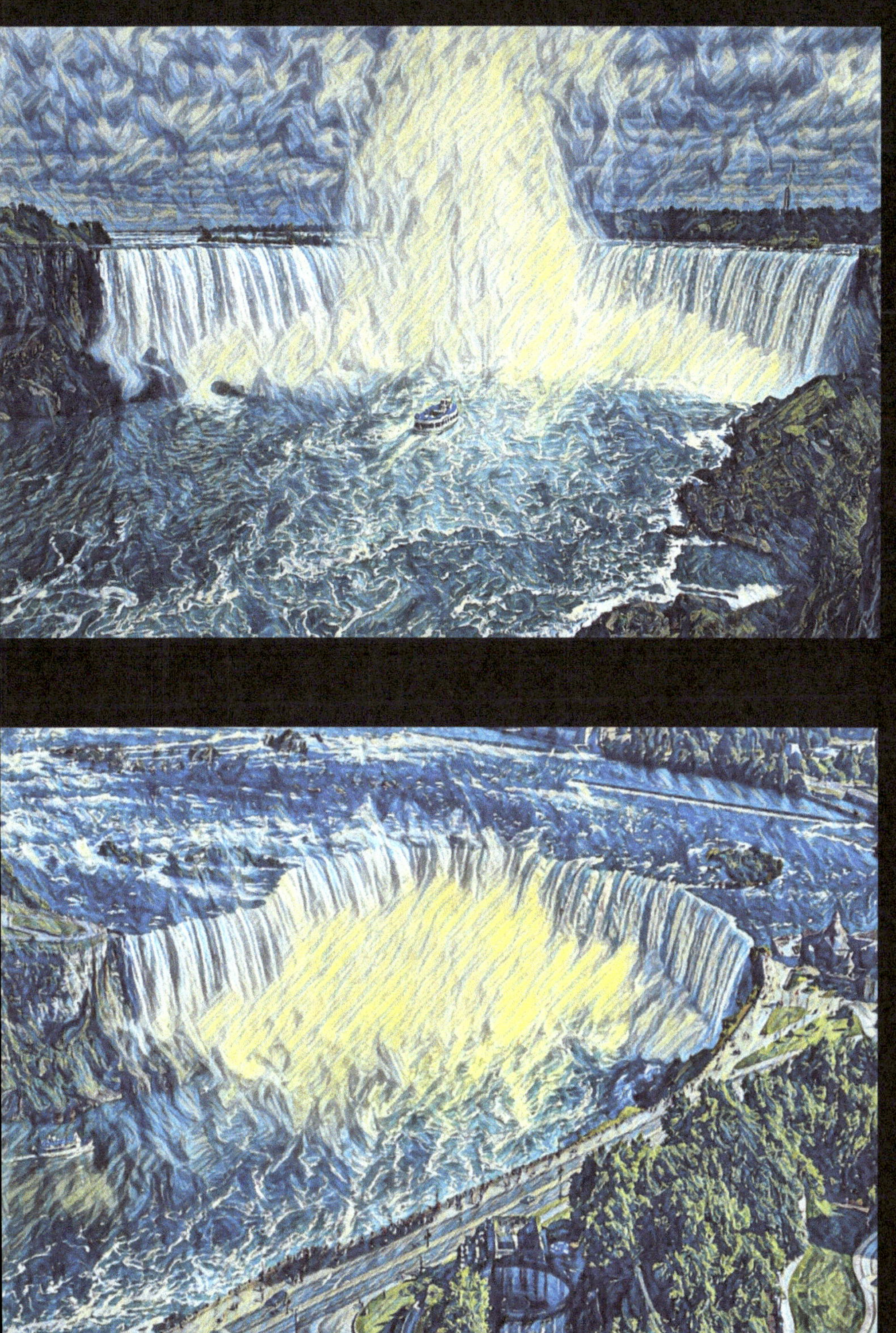

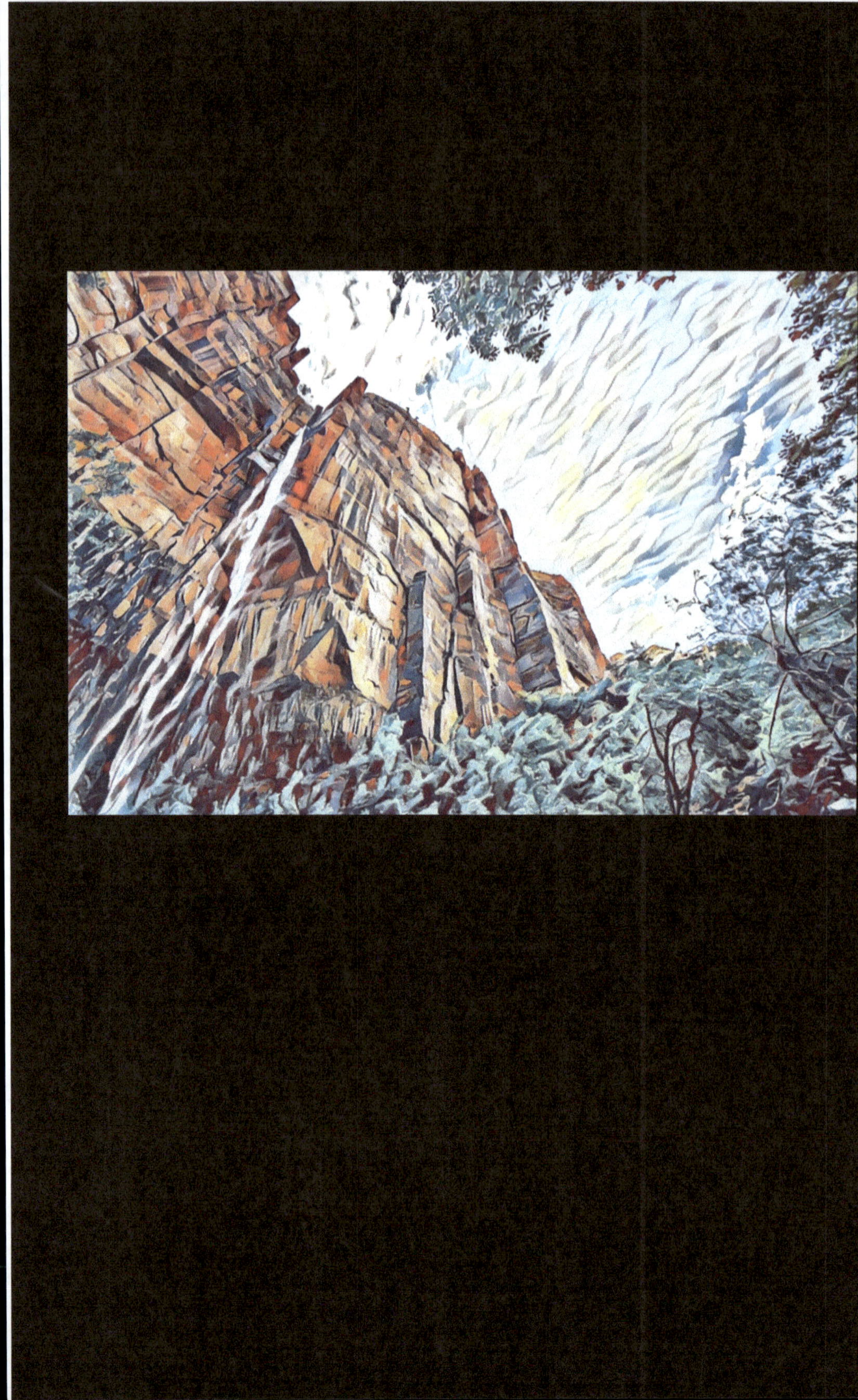

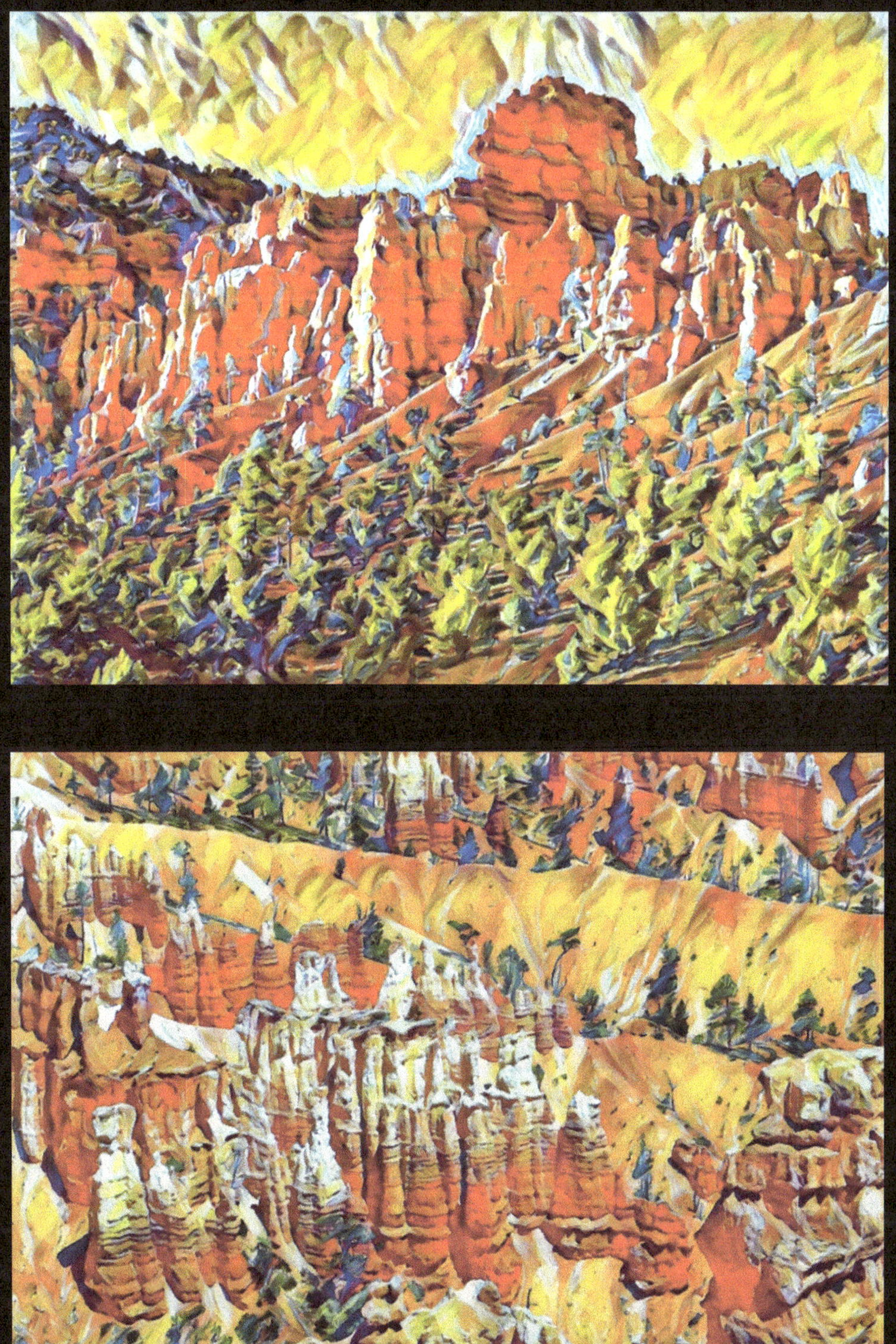

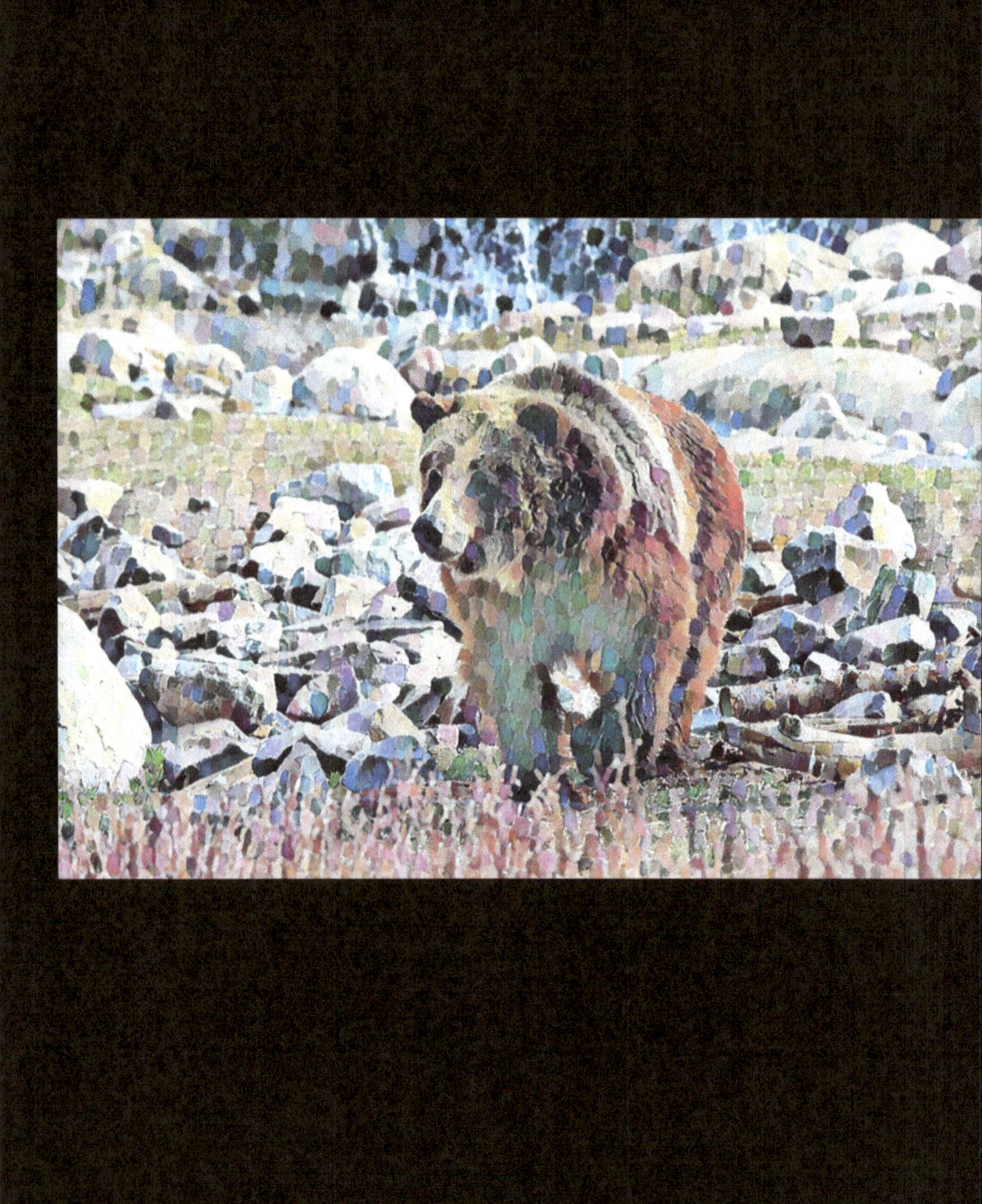

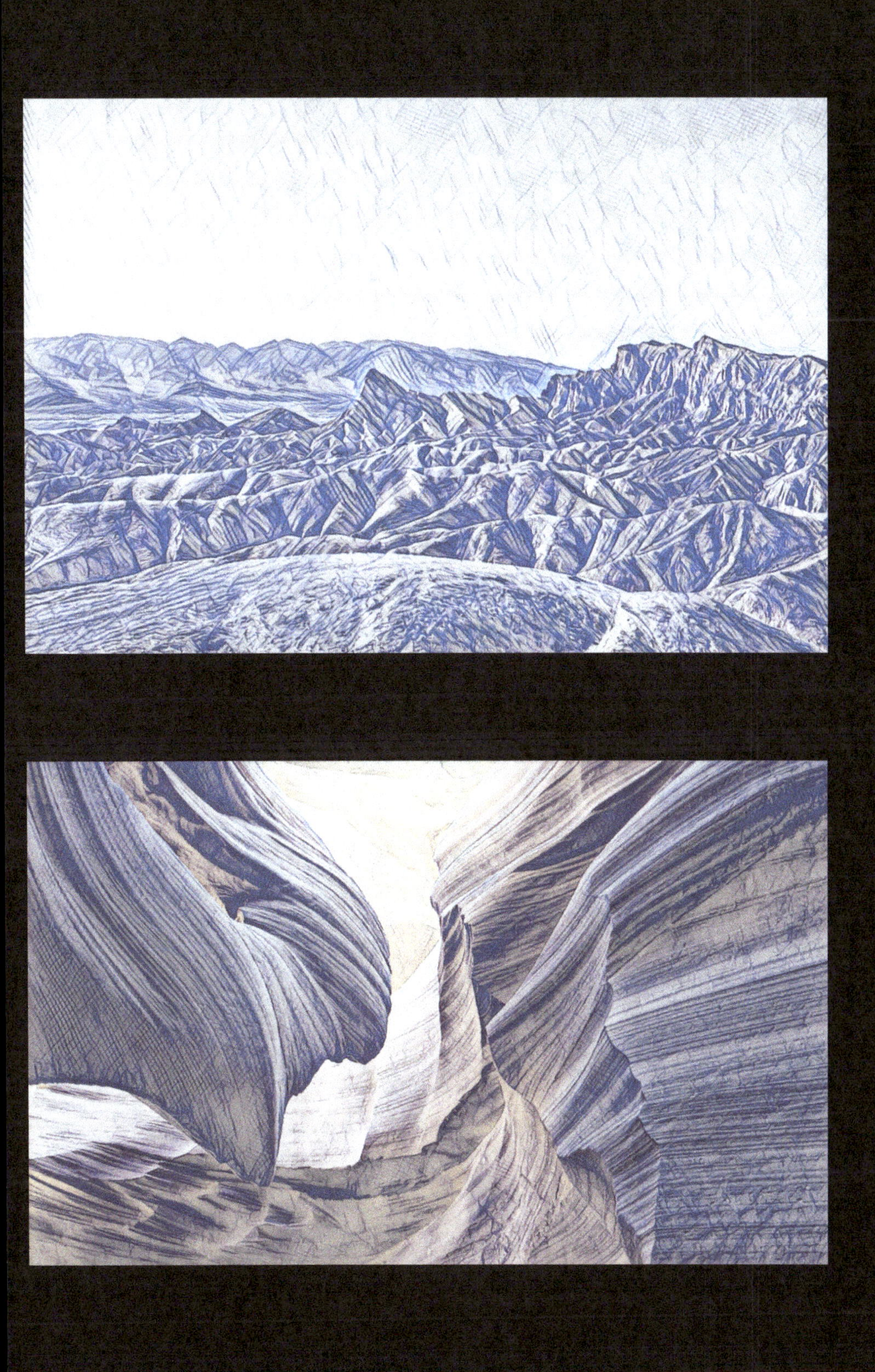

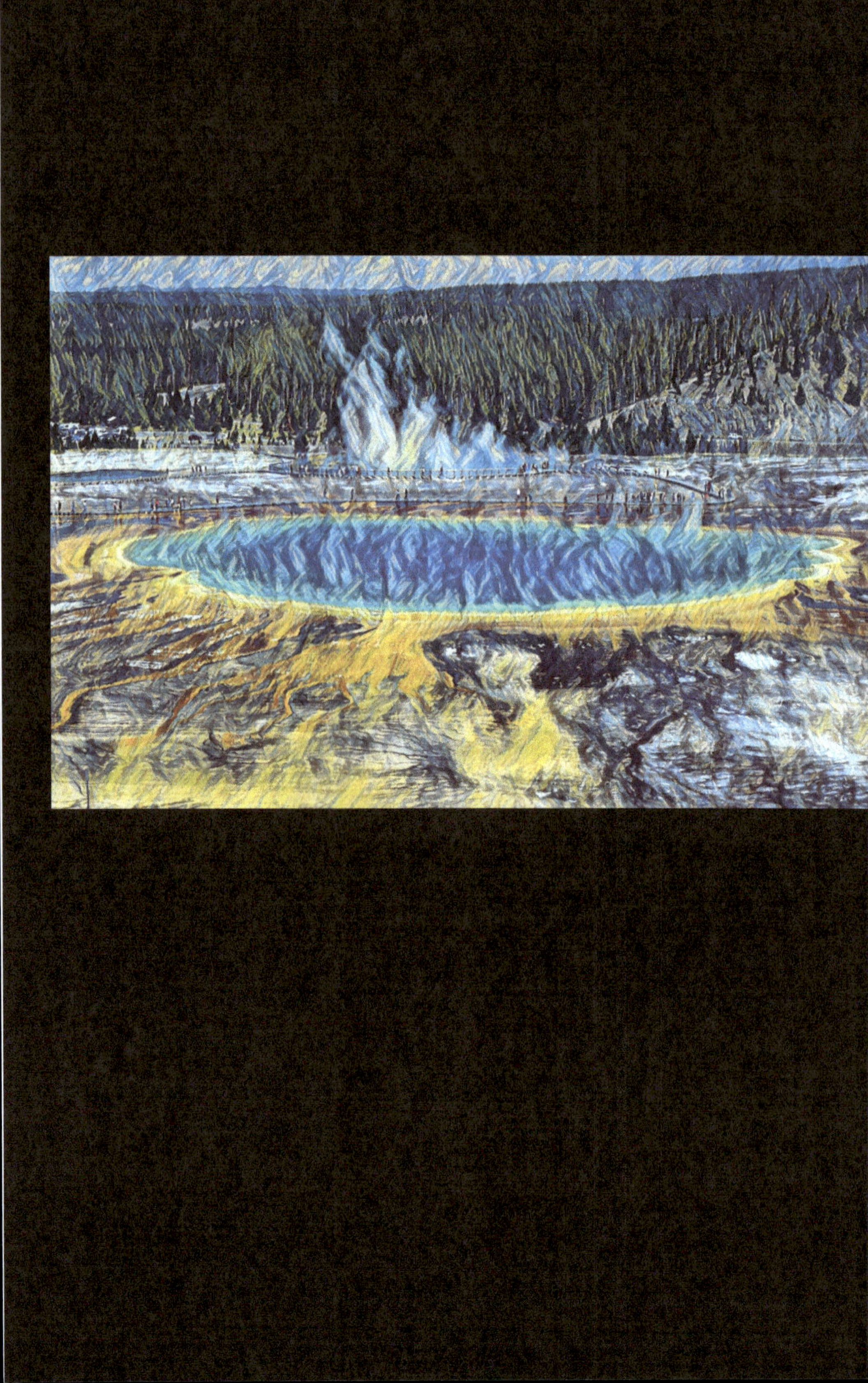

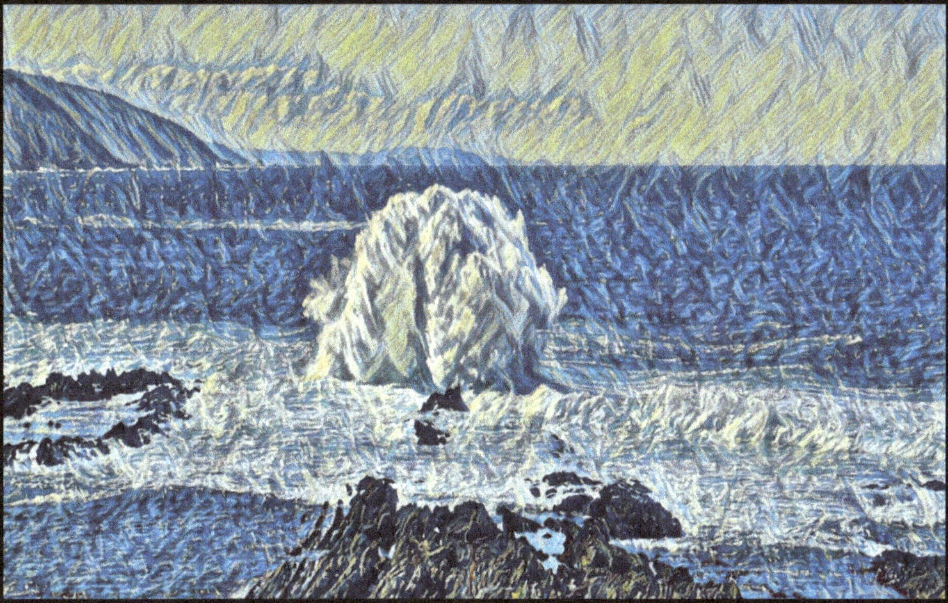

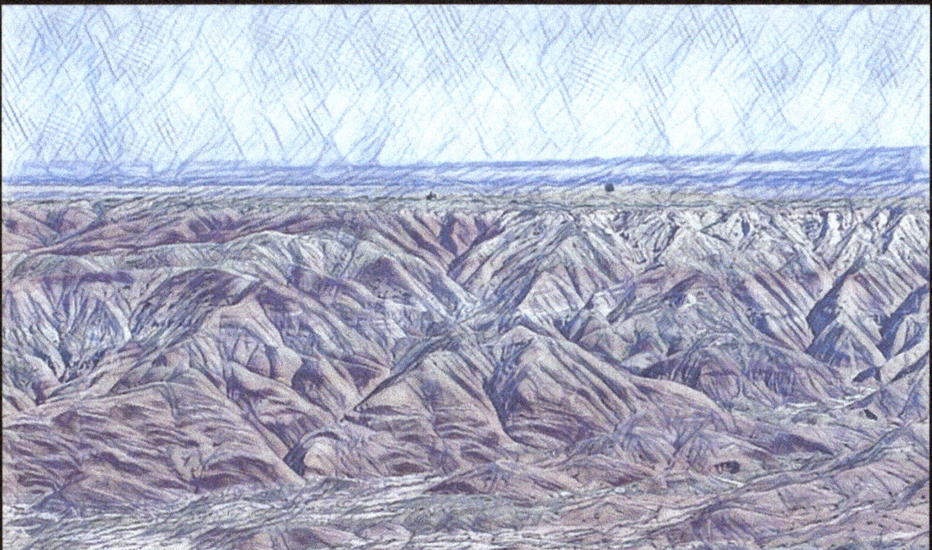

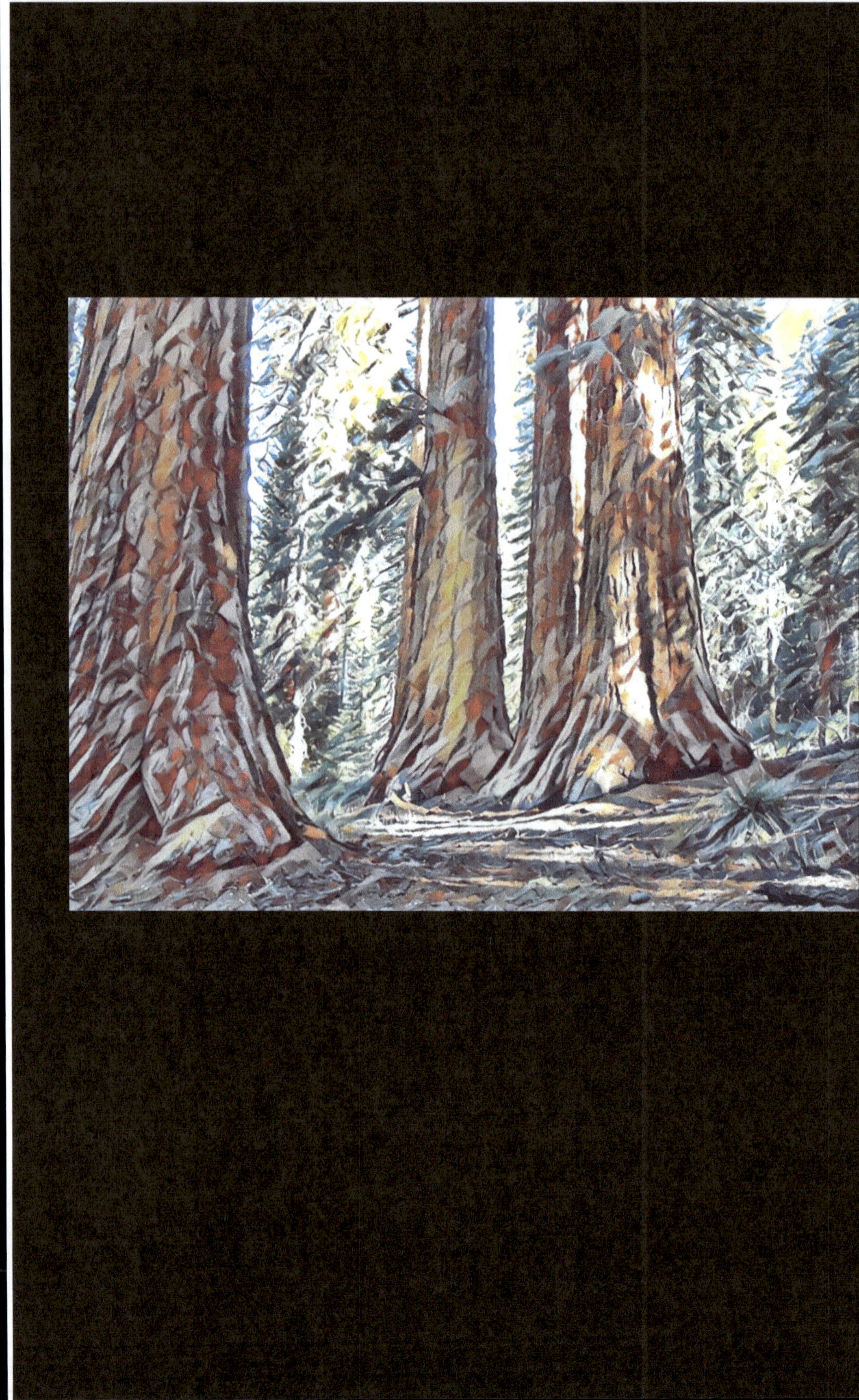

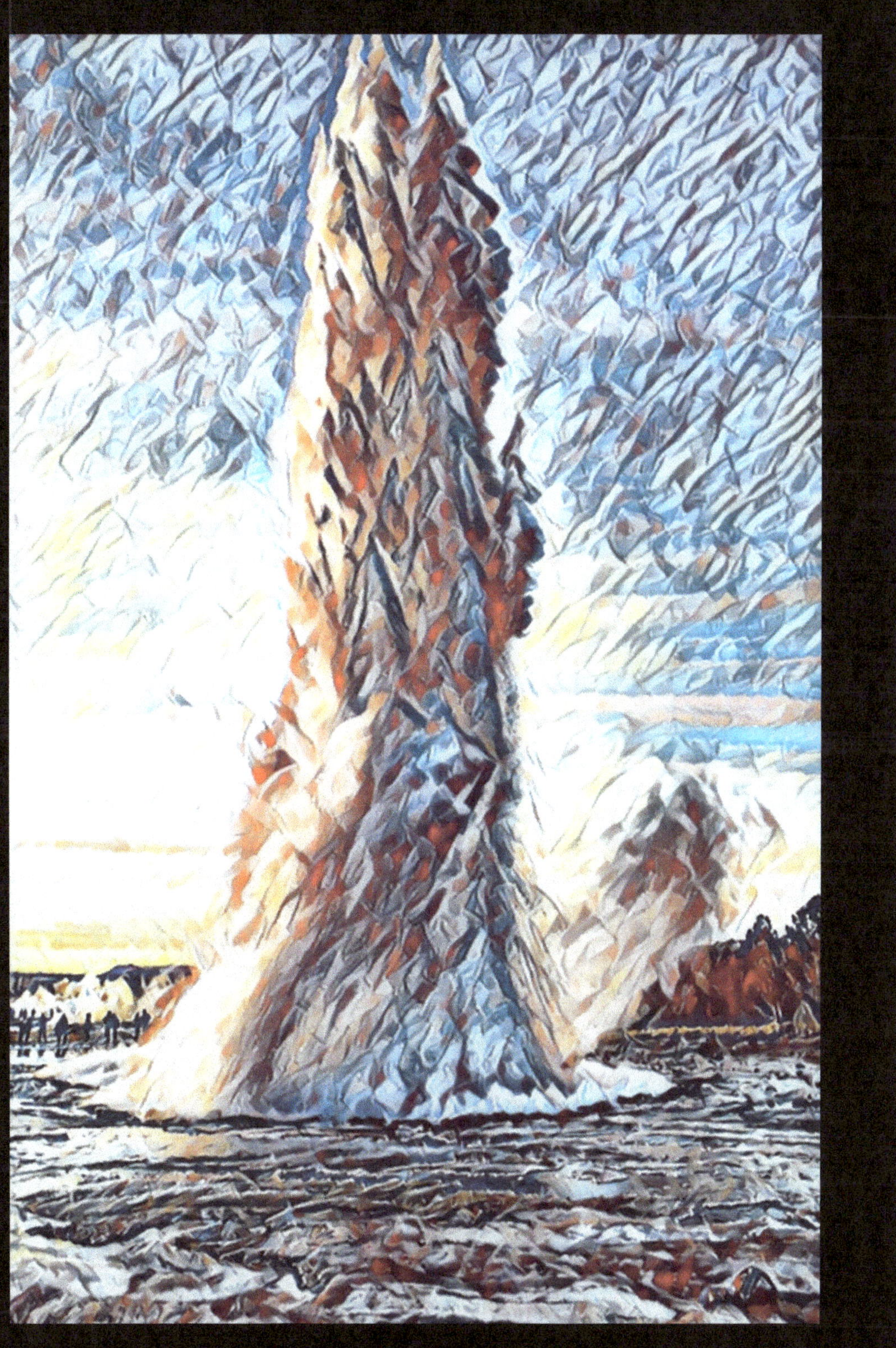

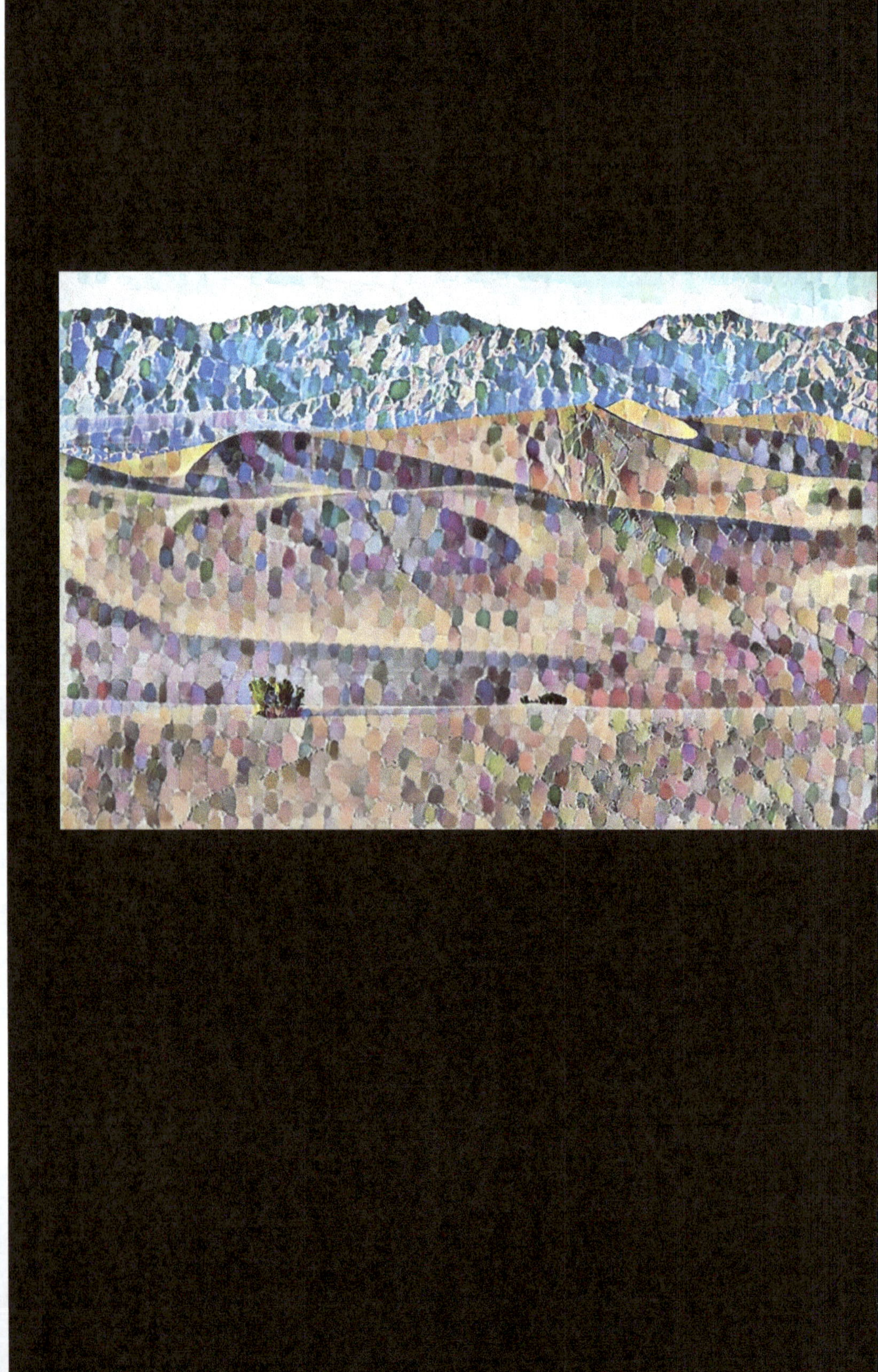

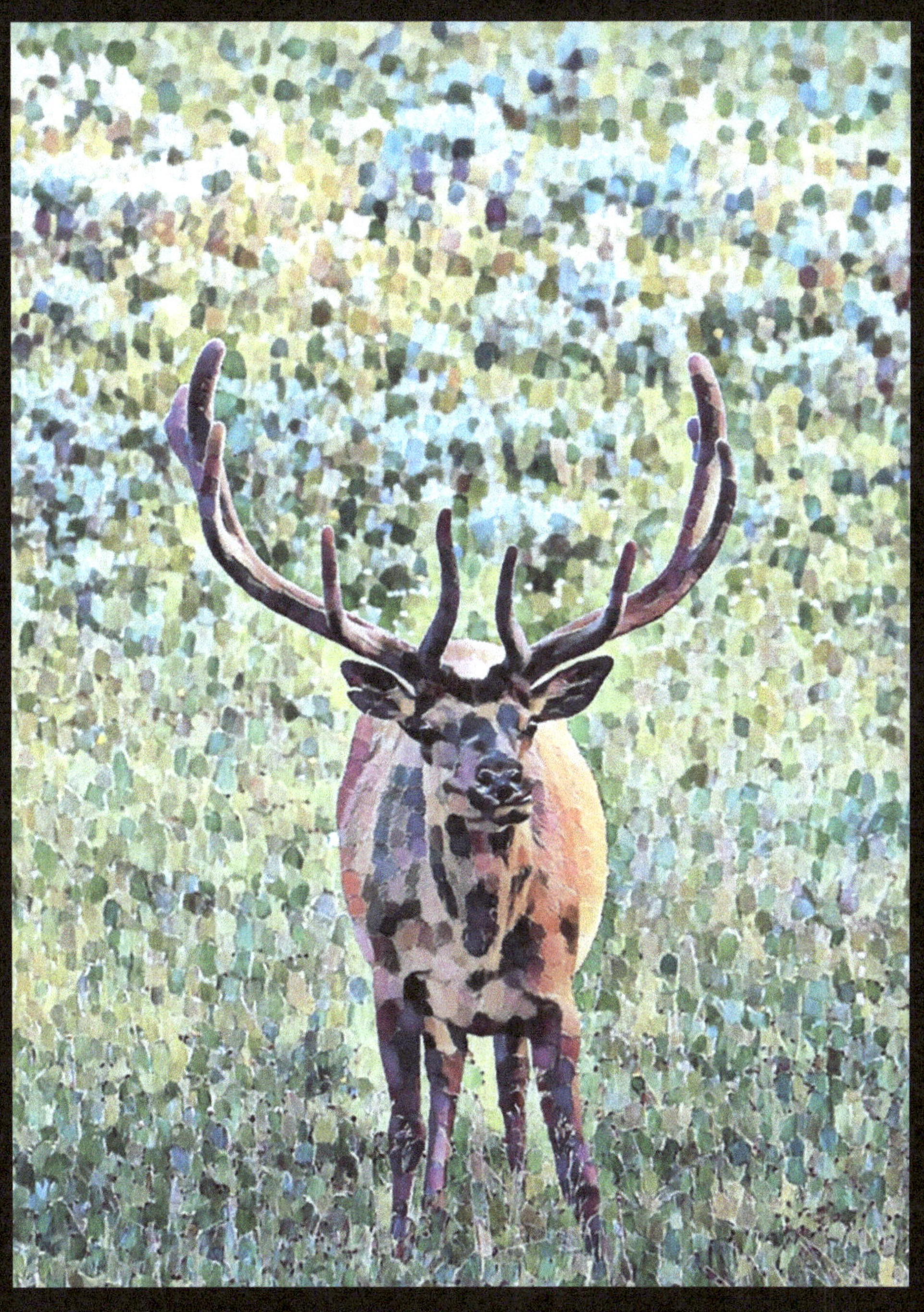

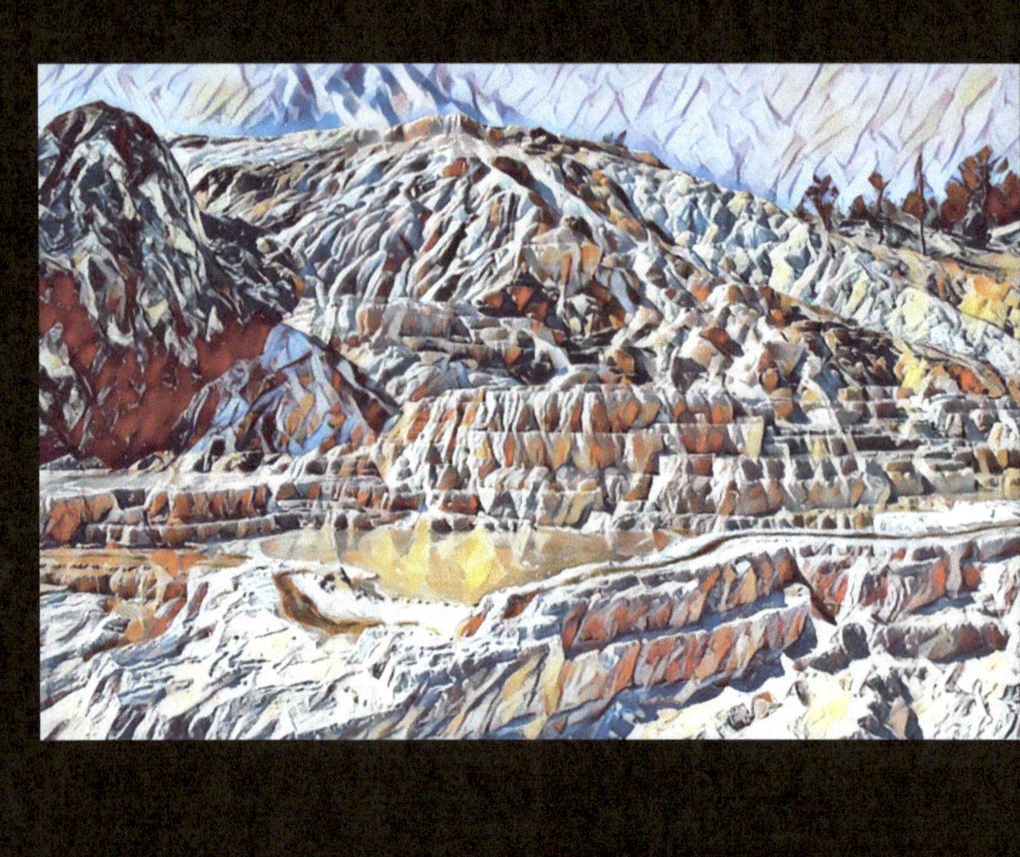

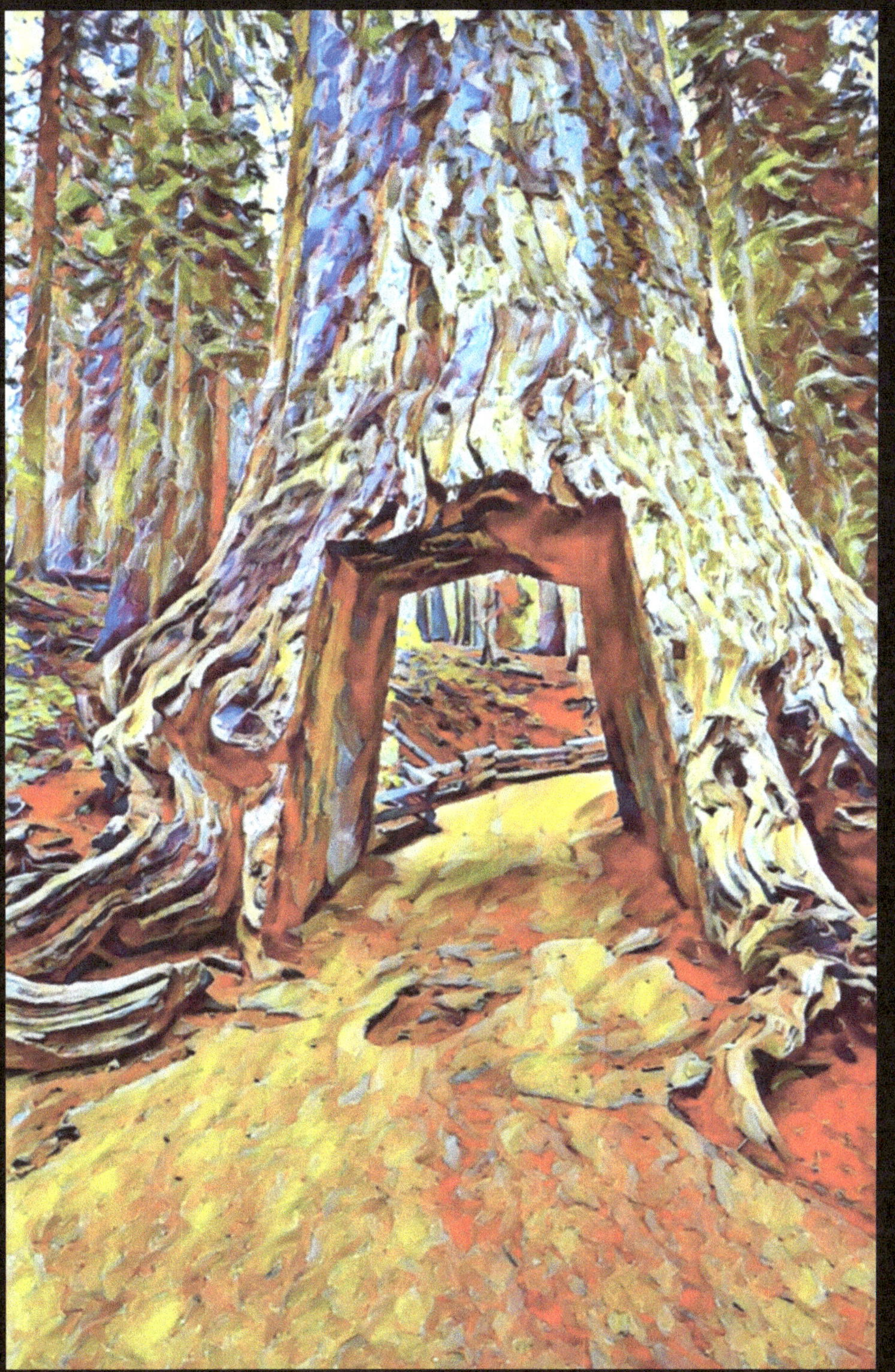

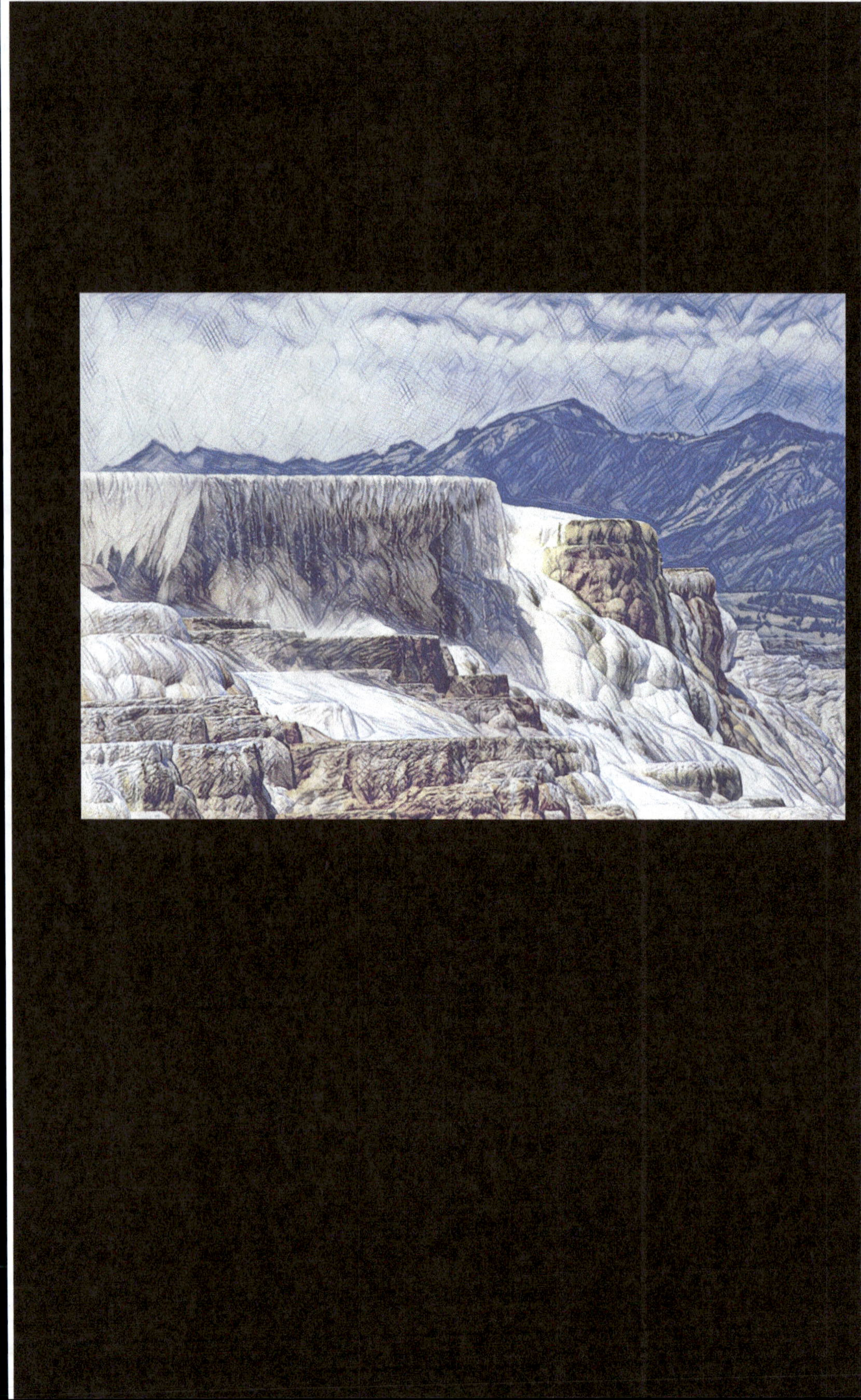

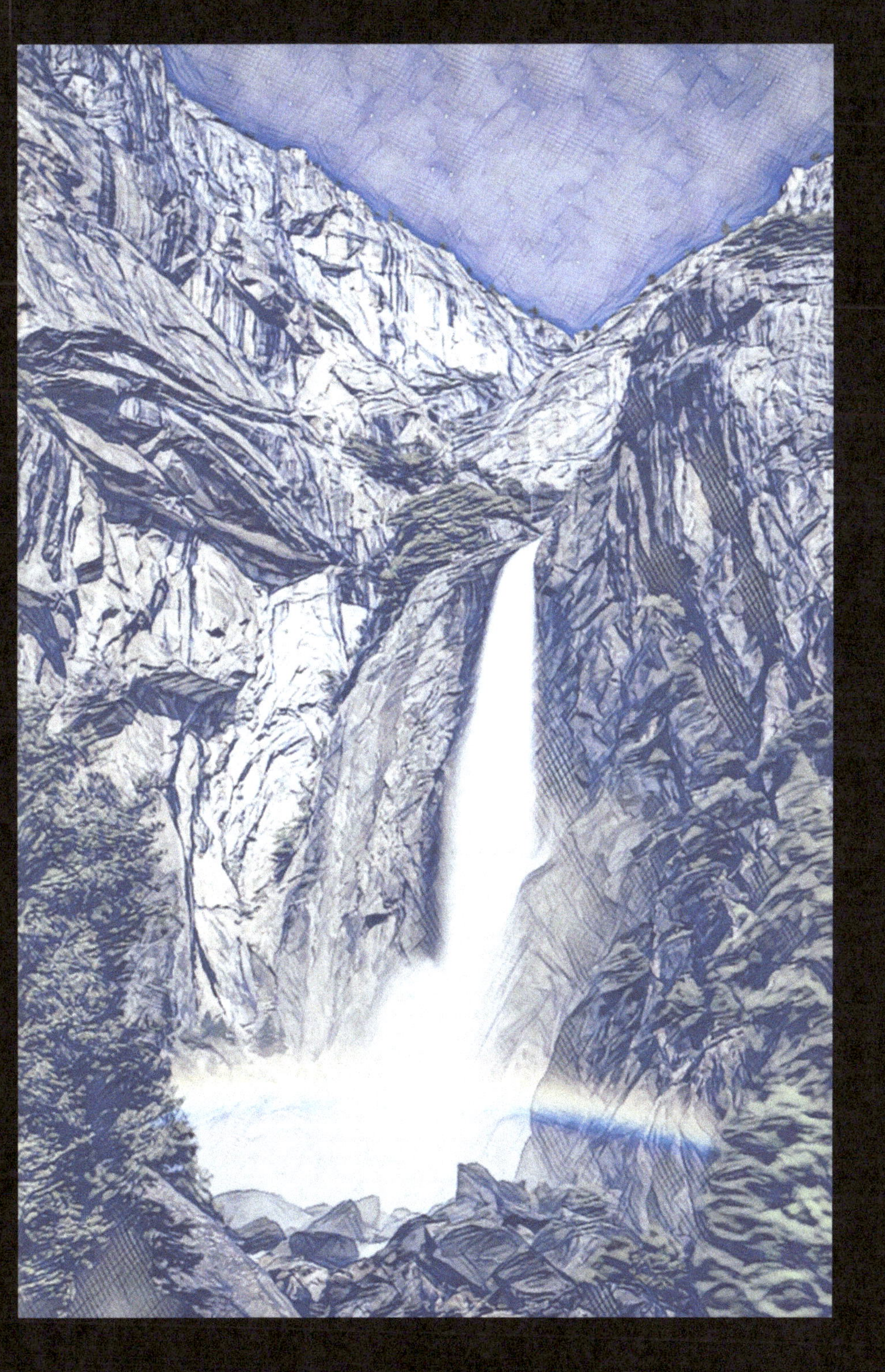

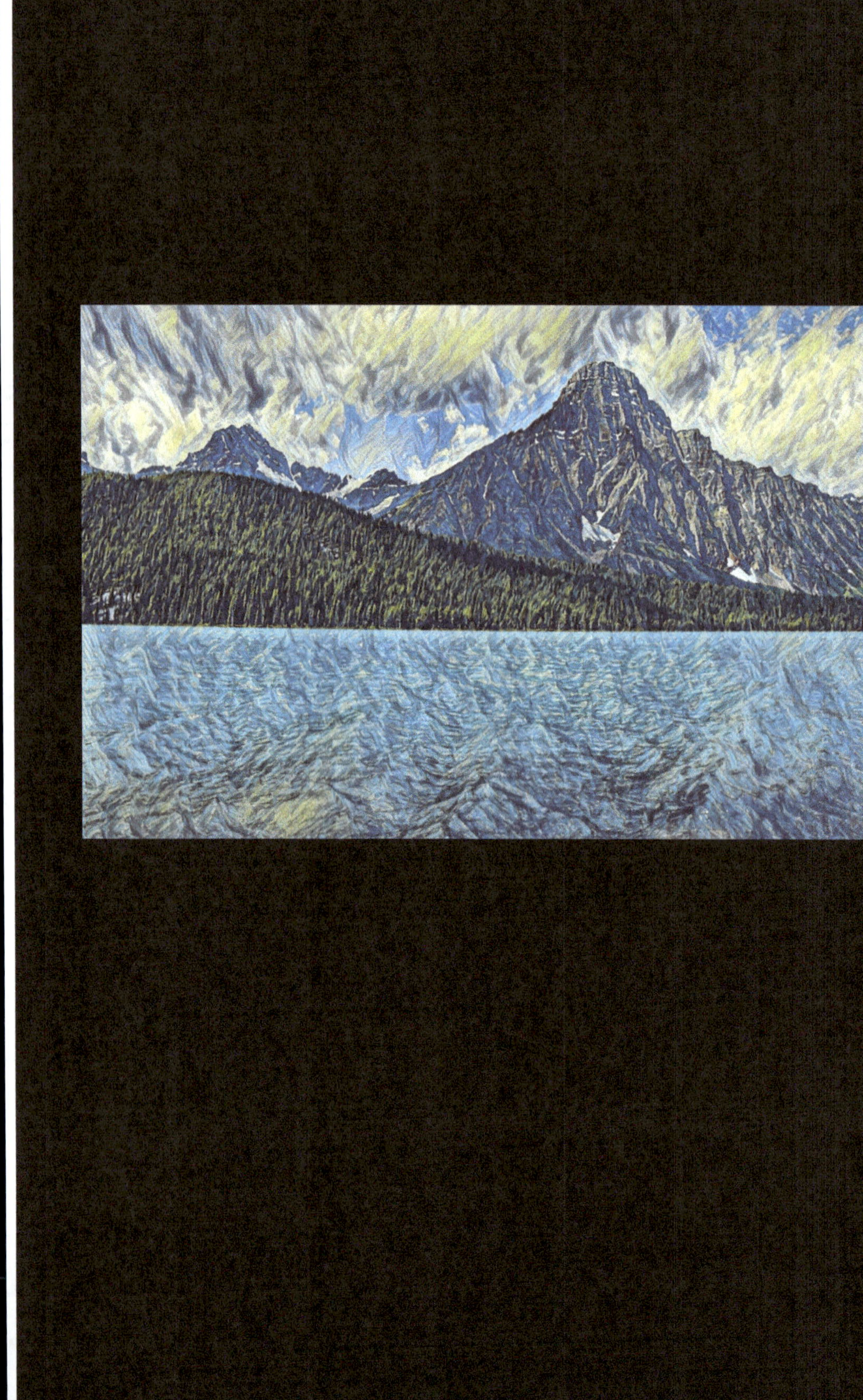

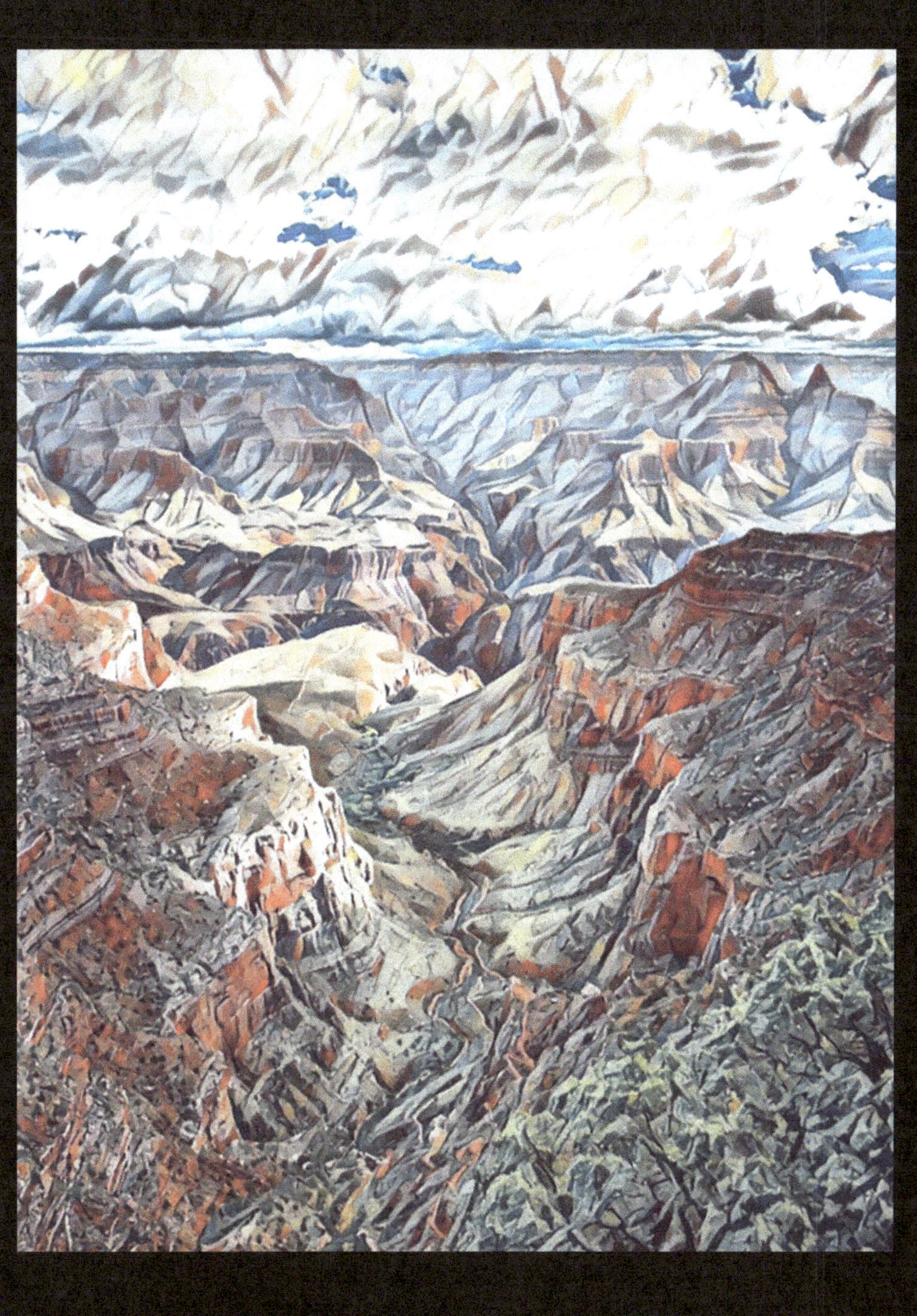

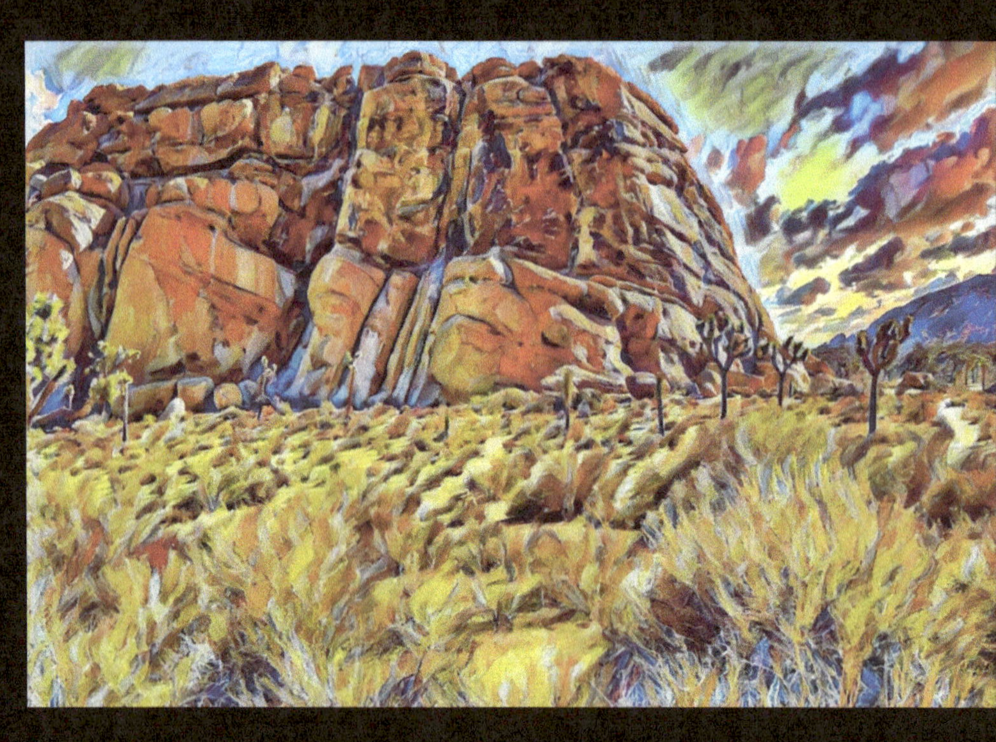

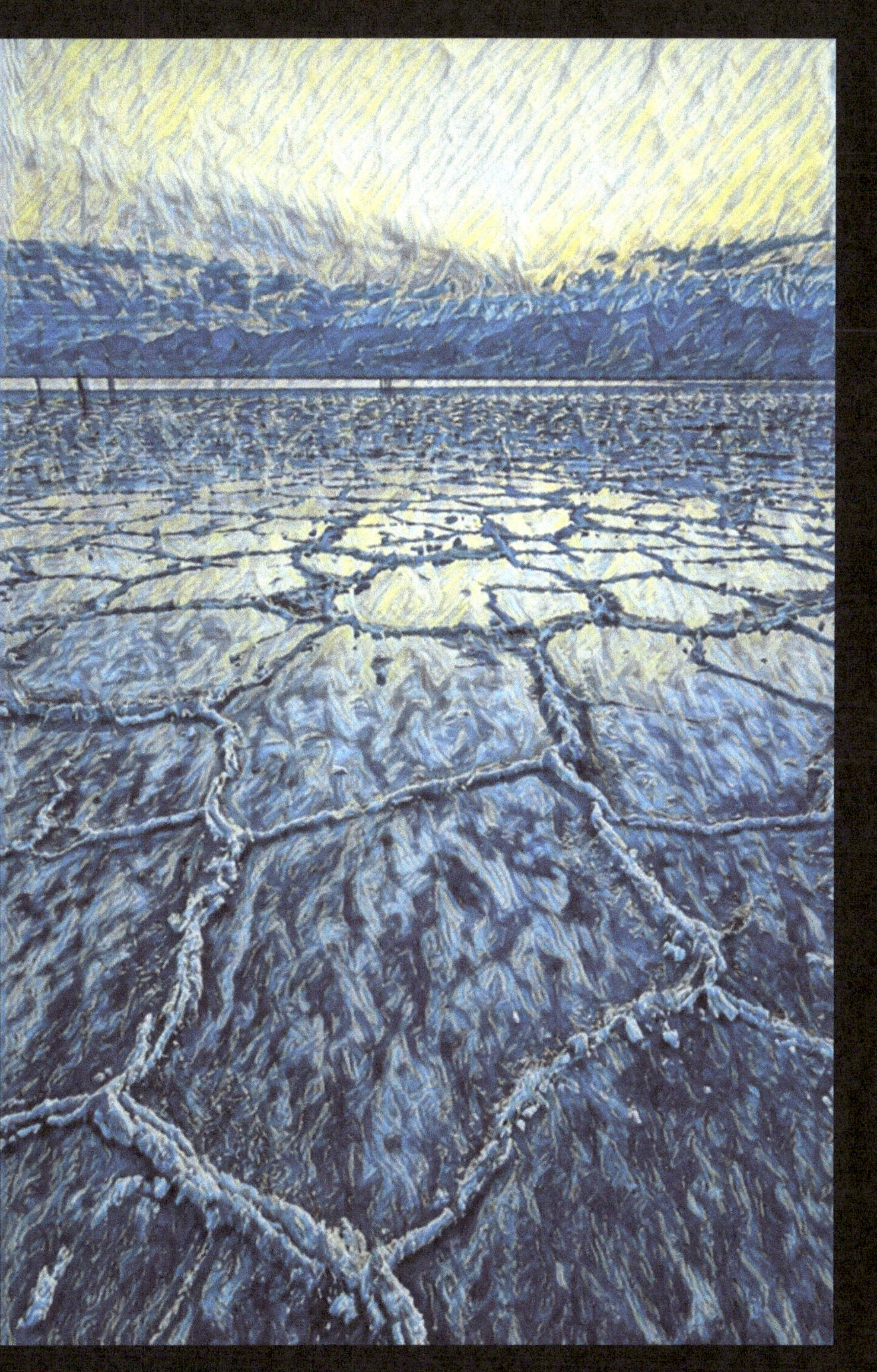

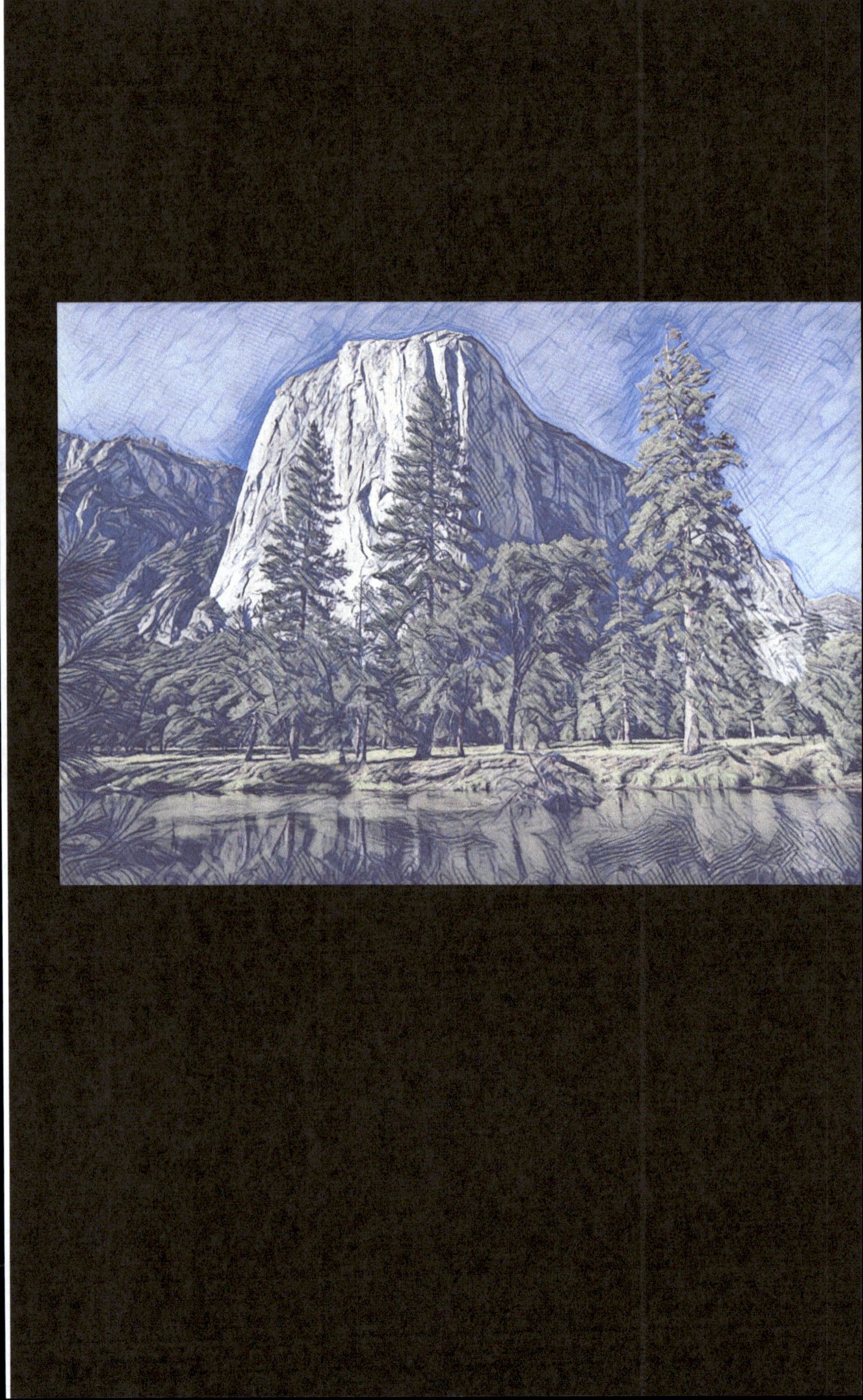

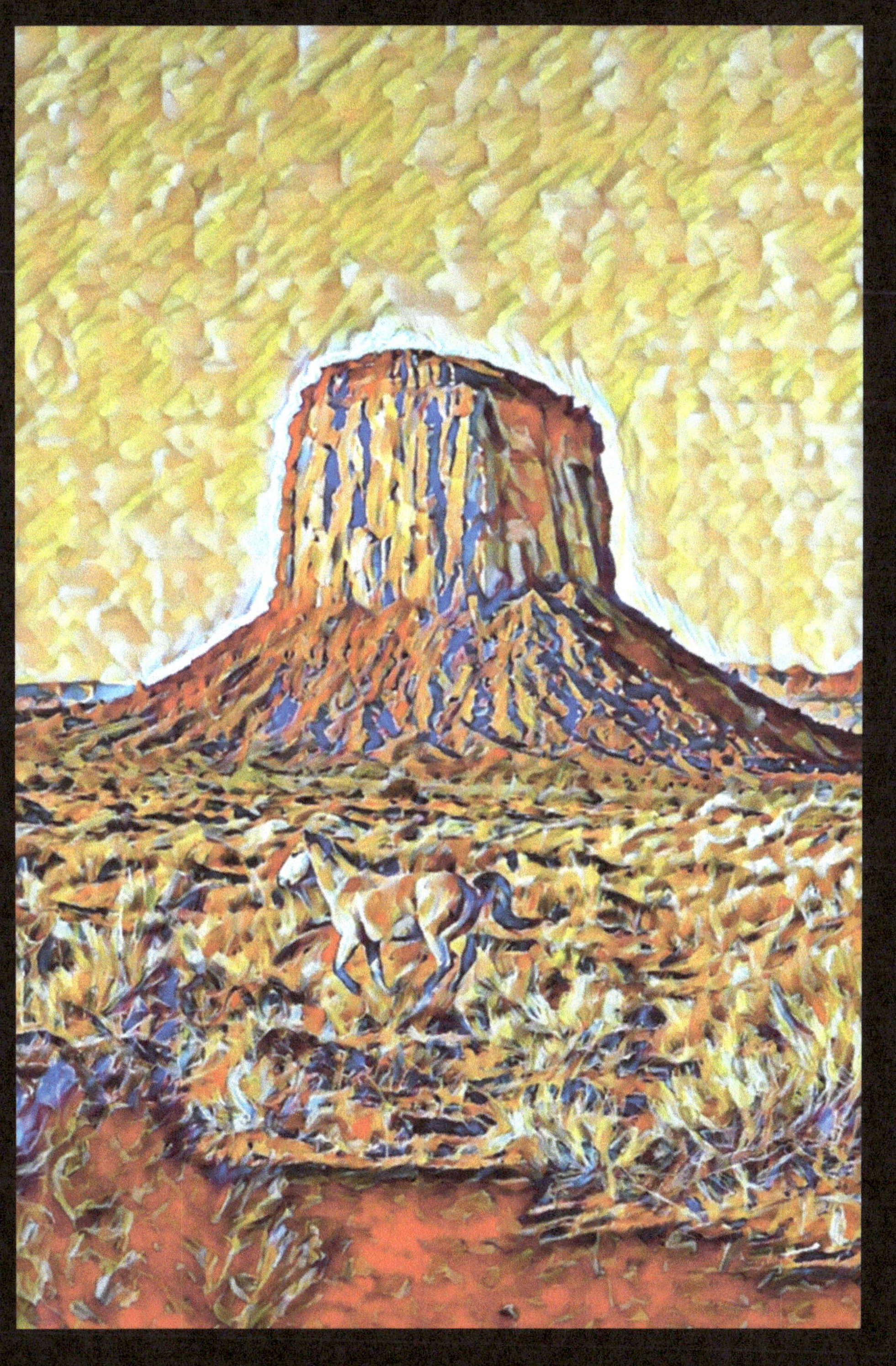

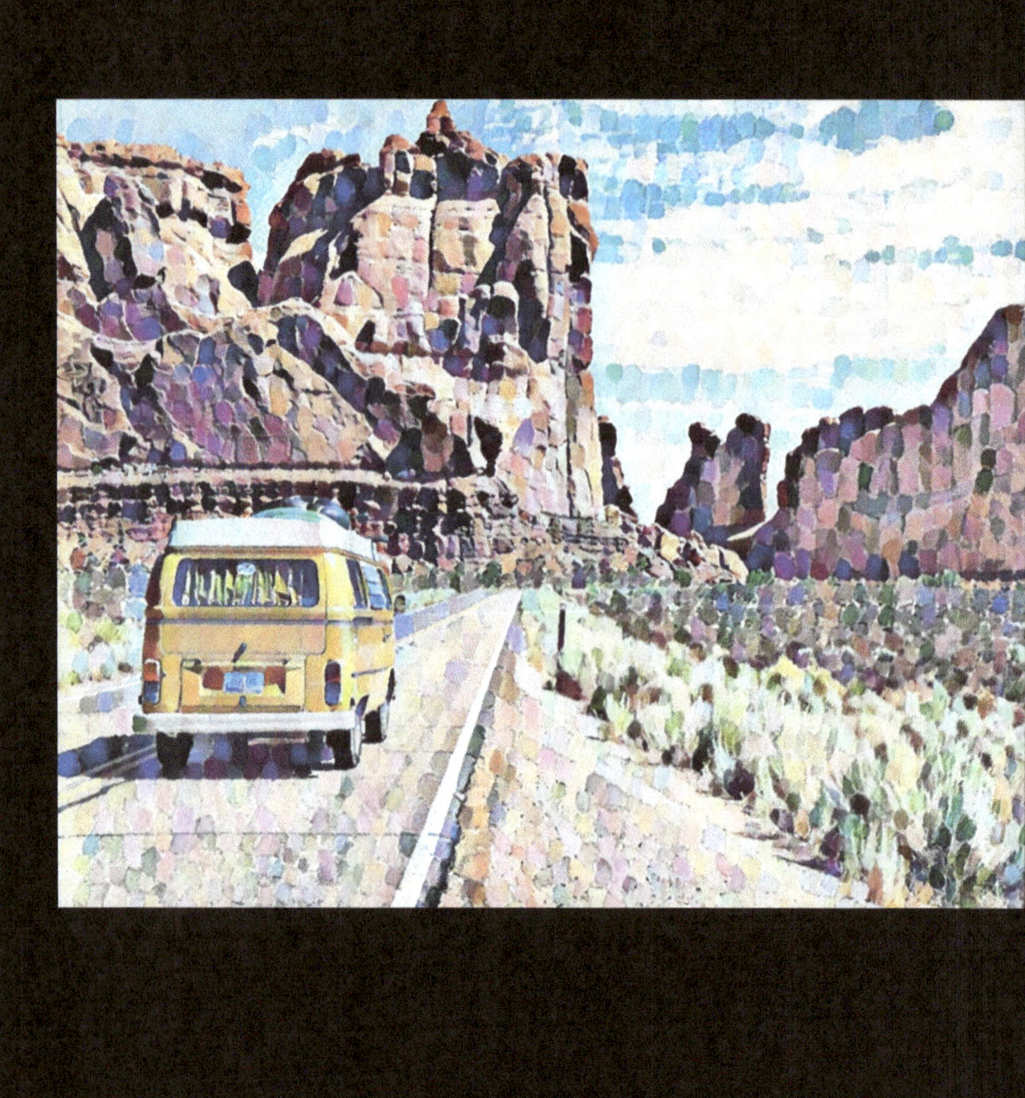

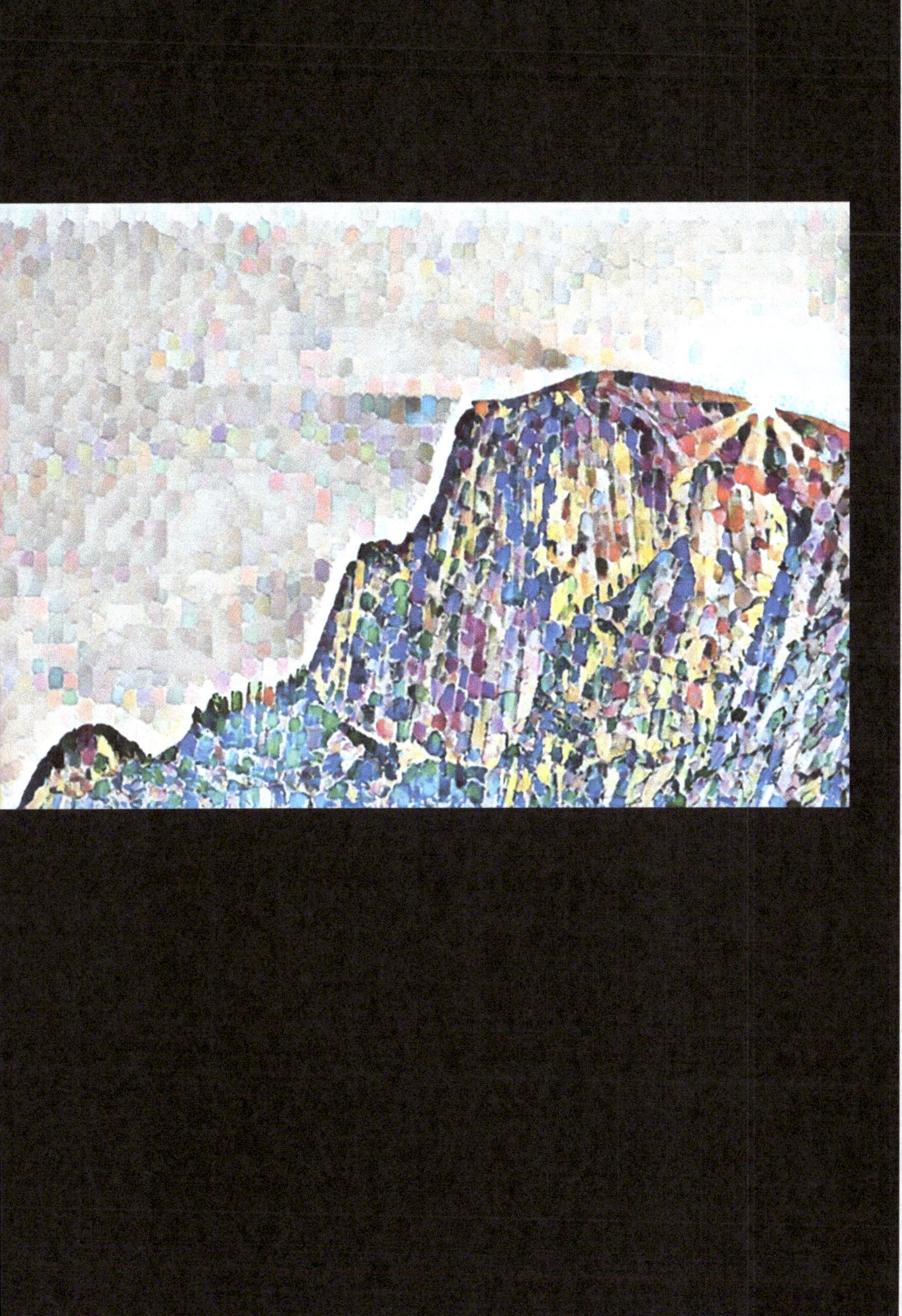

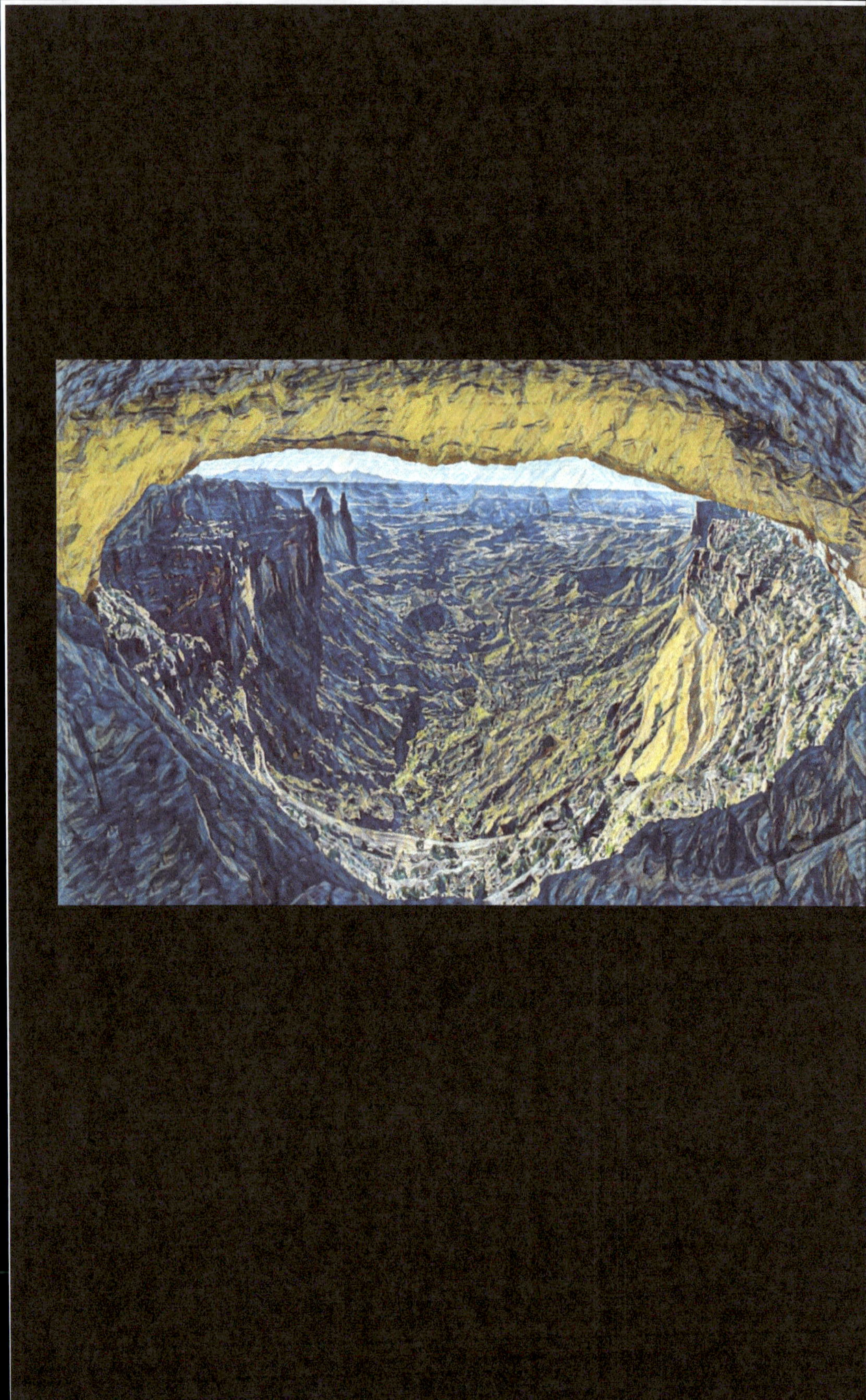

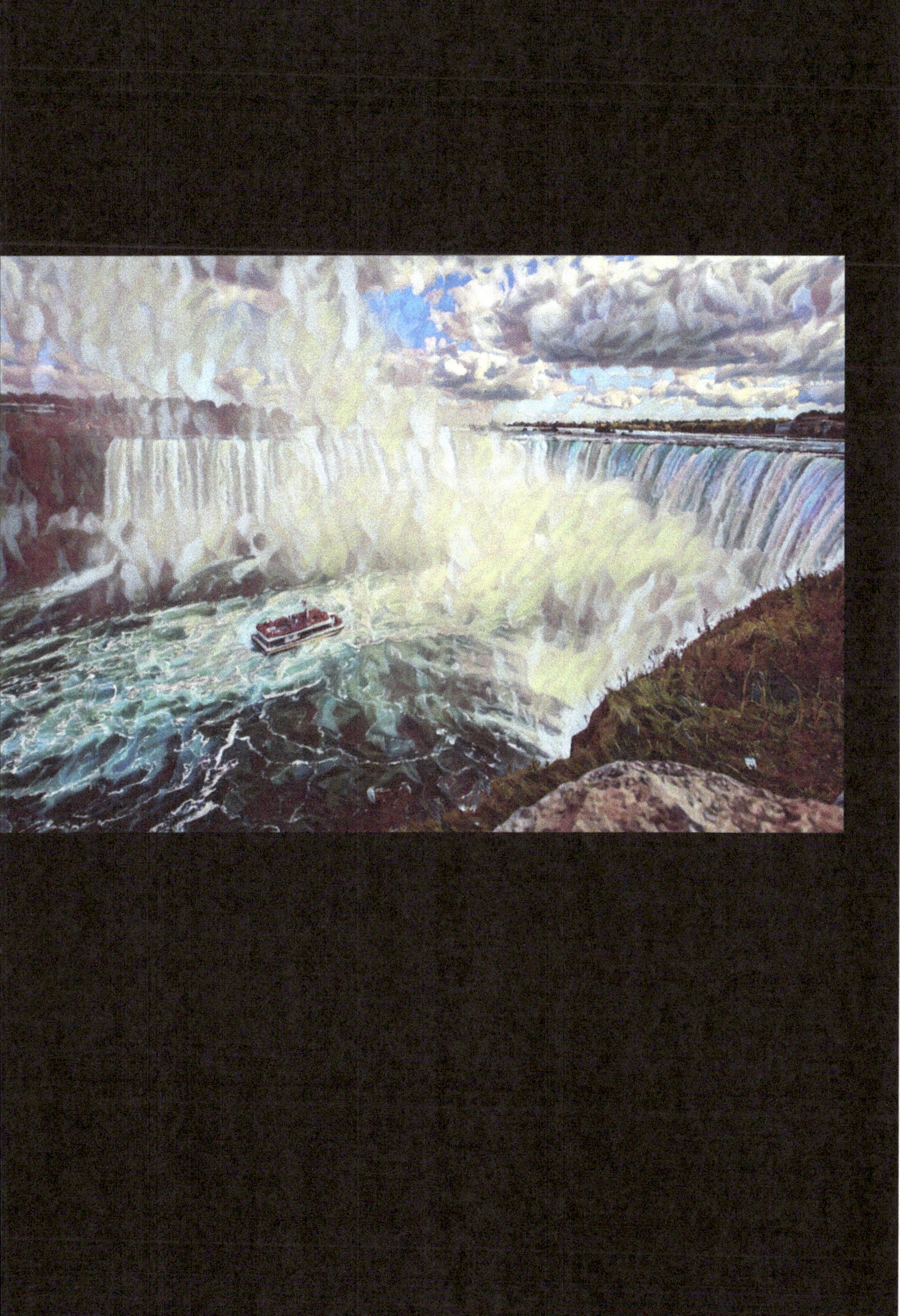

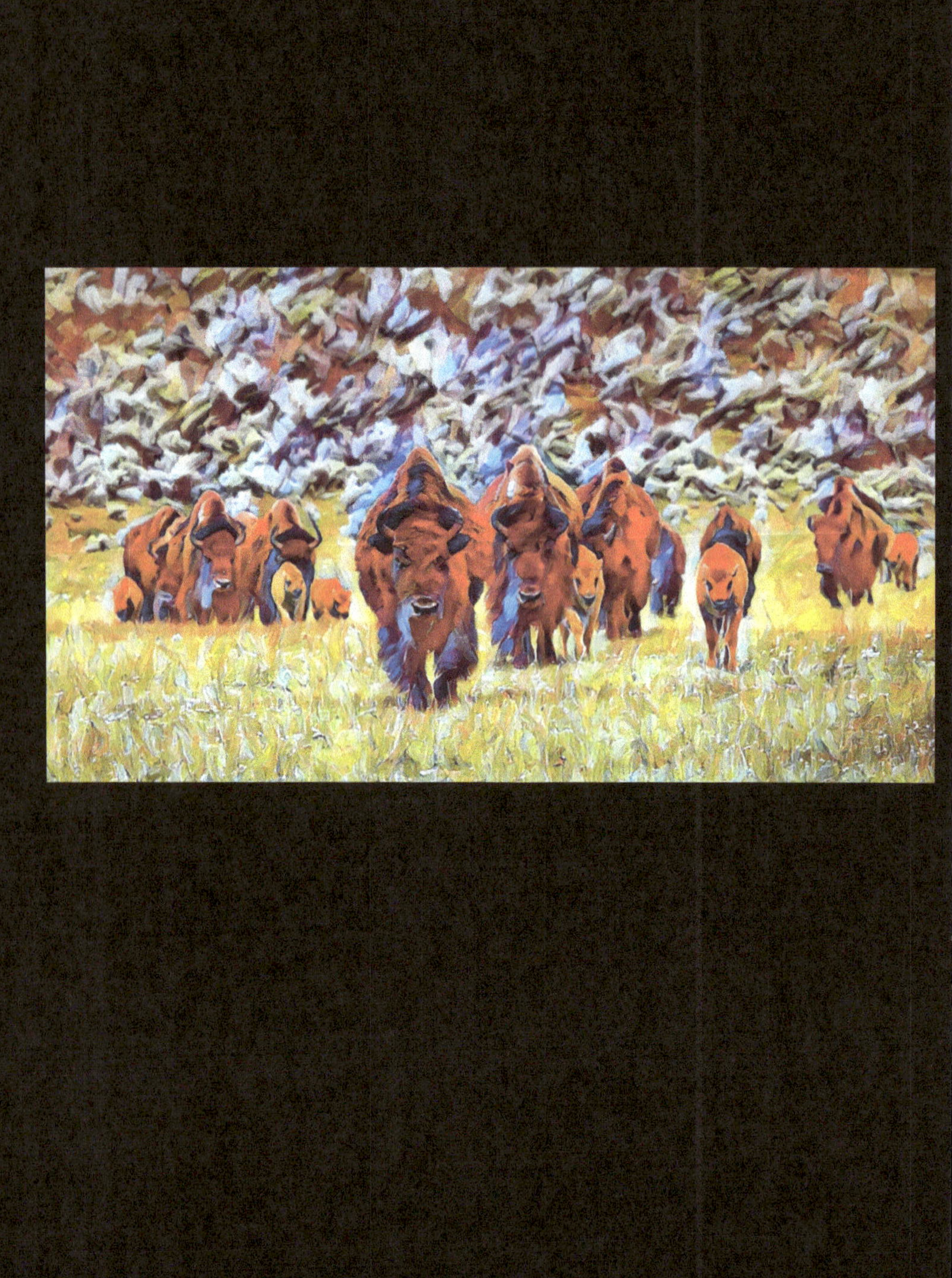

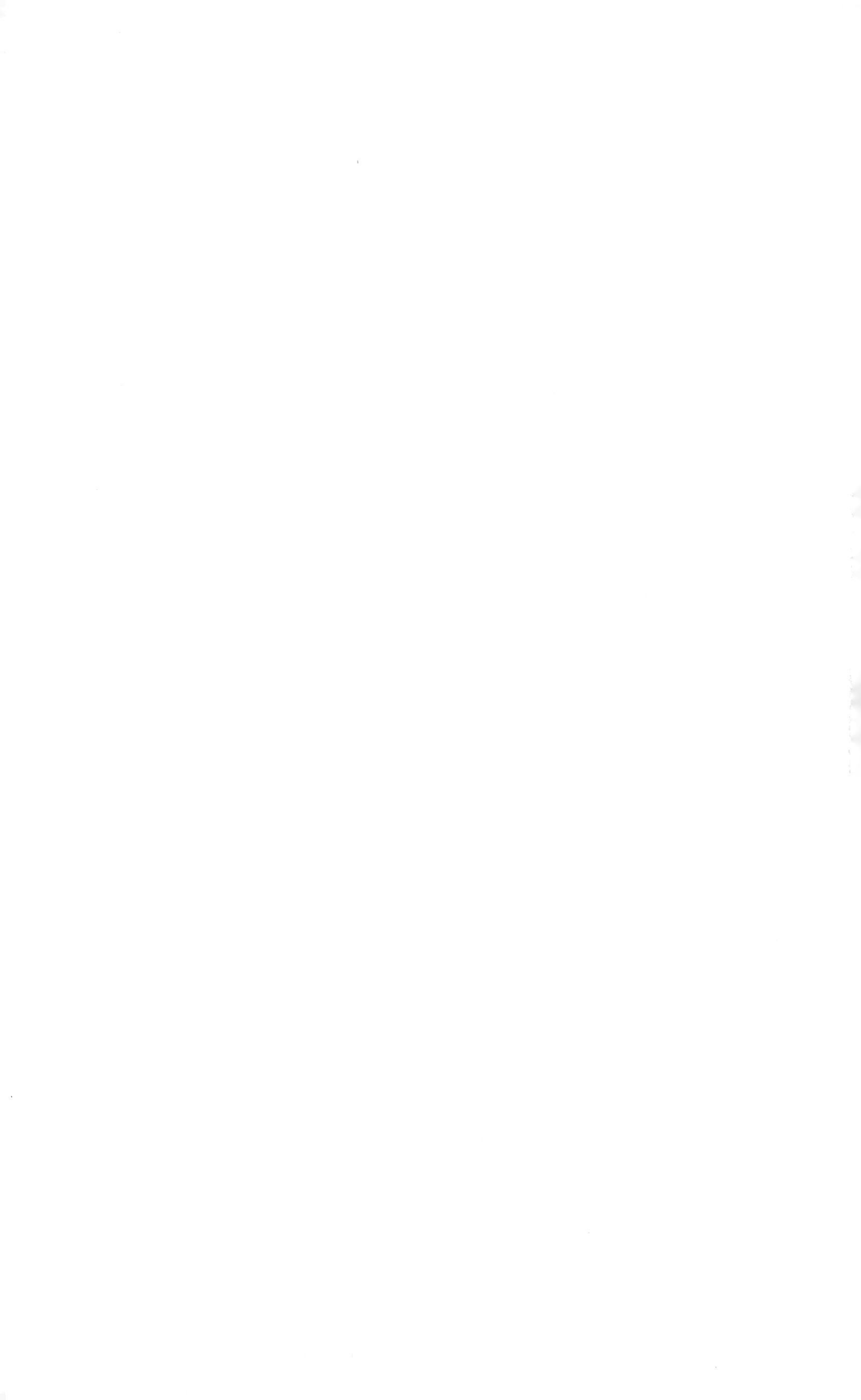

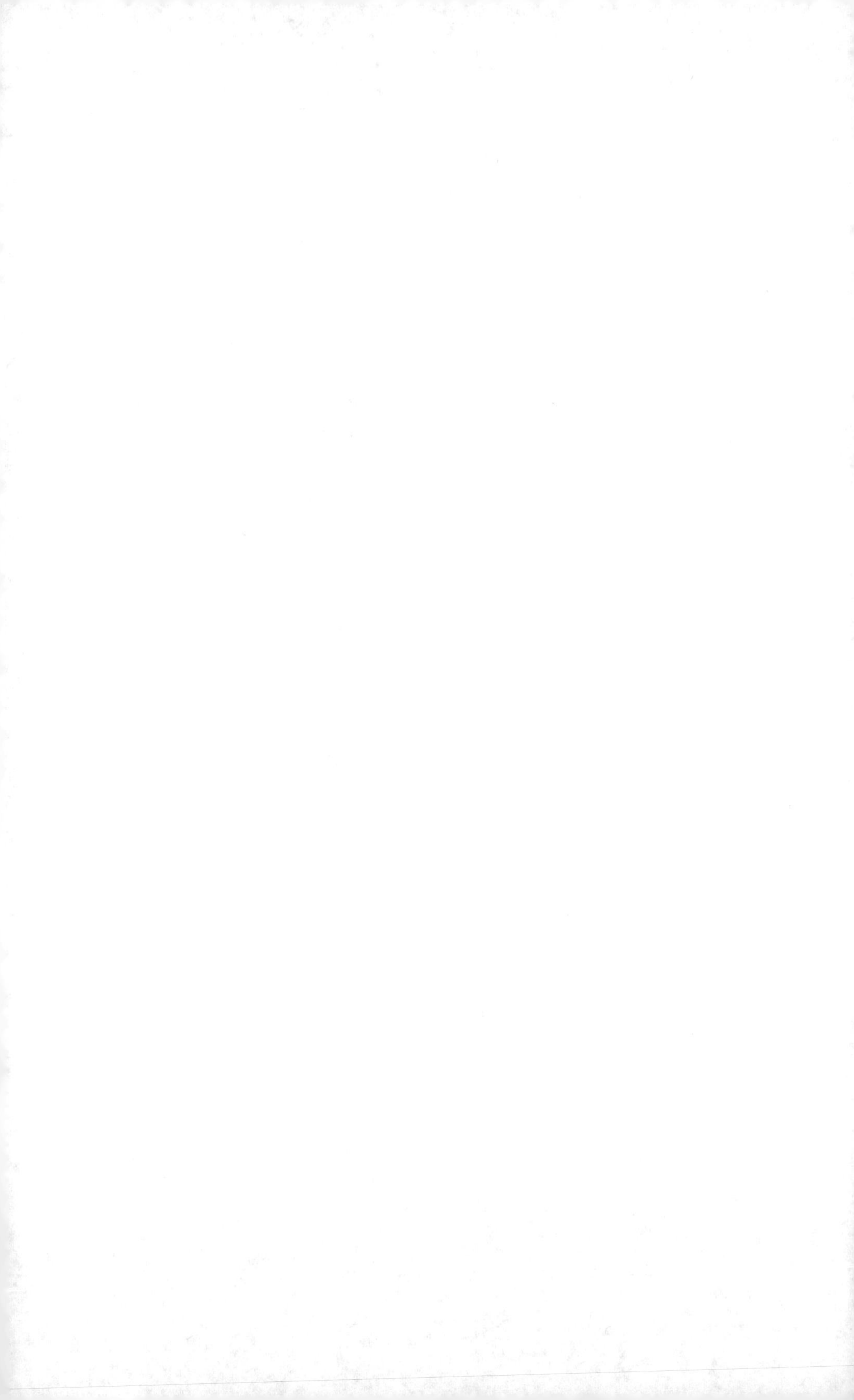